LOVE THROUGH THE DARKNESS

L.M. Wyandotte

L.M. Wyandotte
LOVE THROUGH THE DARKNESS
Published by L.M. Wyandotte

Copyright © 2024 by L.M. Wyandotte

First Edition
ISBN 979-8-218-49950-1

All rights reserved under International and Pan-American Copyright Conventions. Manufactured in the United States.

No part of this publication may be reproduced, stored in or introduced into a retrieval system, or transmitted in any form or by any means (electronic, mechanical, photocopying, recording or otherwise) without the prior written permission of the publisher. This book is sold subject to the condition that it shall not, by way of trade or otherwise, be lent, resold, hired out, or otherwise circulated without the publisher's prior written consent in any form of binding, cover, or condition other than that in which it was published.

L.M. WYANDOTTE

this book is dedicated to the most important people: those who have loved me, those who have hurt me, those who have helped me, and those who have experienced life with me. without all of you, this book would not have been possible.

LOVE THROUGH THE DARKNESS

also by L.M. Wyandotte:

crown confessions vol. 1
crown confessions vol. 2
crown confessions vol. 3

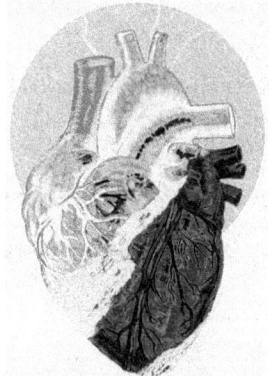

instagram: @l.m.wyandotte
twitter: @lmwyandotte
TikTok: @l.m.wyandotte
Facebook: L.M. Wyandotte

L.M. WYANDOTTE

too many people want to get away from
their life. however, unless you keep moving
and never settle, the problems
will be wherever you left when you get back.

i'm done learning life lessons at this

point in my life.

L.M. WYANDOTTE

i'm not sure what the worst part of the day is: knowing she didn't spend it with me or knowing she spent it with him.

days are spent wondering if my next day

will have more of her in it.

L.M. WYANDOTTE

the sunshine warms me.
the sunshine brightens my day.
the sunshine helps me grow.
i can't hold her. but, she is my sunshine.

LOVE THROUGH THE DARKNESS

i love you means a lot. but, have you ever had someone tell you "i would give my life for yours."? that's deeper than love. love gets you to a point in a connection. however, when someone tells you they value your life more than theirs, you should never need to question your importance to them. that is the best definition of being all in and committed.

L.M. WYANDOTTE

in her eyes i could do no wrong. but, i did the worst wrong of all because i couldn't save her.

i am hers. all that i am. everything from my breath to my flesh. all i need from her, is her hand and to tell me i get to be with her.

L.M. WYANDOTTE

for her, i am zeus and sunshine.

for her, i am cotton and shade.

for her, i am whatever she needs.

i am forever in debt to her.
no amount of love i give will repay
what she has given me. i hope the
interest continues to grow.

L.M. WYANDOTTE

sit with me. let's have a drink.
let us compare who has the best
shittier life. i'll let you go first.

LOVE THROUGH THE DARKNESS

my heart is heavy with the weight of
stories i don't want to share.

L.M. WYANDOTTE

i feel all the feelings because of her.

LOVE THROUGH THE DARKNESS

she makes me want to be a better man. not
just for myself. for her. because i know
she deserves that. she deserves better
than me and that's why i make the effort
to be better each day.

L.M. WYANDOTTE

she treated my scribbles as if they were exquisite pieces of art. her way of treasuring the art that reflected my soul struck me as a sign. a sign she was my person.

LOVE THROUGH THE DARKNESS

there are days whiskey poses the questions.
and nights it provides the answers.

pain and love are meant to remind you of
being human. feeling both at the same time
cause you to feel as if you could be a
greek god. afterwards.

her eyes can tell me more about her

emotions than words can.

L.M. WYANDOTTE

sad days & nights bring strong days & nights.
they are just not usually back to back.

still trying to figure out who i am. i imagine this will take my whole life.

L.M. WYANDOTTE

each day waking up next to her reminds
me, i've won the love lottery.

the beach is always peaceful, even in a storm. that's how i wished people saw me.

my love for her even scares me. i can't tell her all the things i'd do for her because i'm still learning who she is.

so many bottles. so many poems.

L.M. WYANDOTTE

billions of women in the world. i only want to love one.

she's gone. i'll never get to hold her
again. maybe one day.

L.M. WYANDOTTE

without the experiences there's no feelings.
without the feelings there's no emotions.
without the emotions there's no poems.
without the poems there's only drinking.

she's my drug. i'm an addict and i don't want to get clean. i want a forever fix.

L.M. WYANDOTTE

without her, i don't exist.

stay away from the deep end. there's no lifeguard on duty.

L.M. WYANDOTTE

why?

clocks will stop. calendars will expire.
but. i'll still be waiting for her.

L.M. WYANDOTTE

i'm not lonely. the bottle is keeping me company until she comes back.

i'm her's. even if she can't be mine.

right now.

i would never sell my soul. it's priceless.
some people have sold their soul and wonder
why life went to shit.

too many triggers around. i try my best
not to lose my shit. but. it happens.
that's why there's so many empty bottles
in the corner.

L.M. WYANDOTTE

i don't care if there's a pot of gold at
the end of the rainbow. just hope there's
some whiskey.

i wonder how many millionaires hate they
can afford a gun and a bullet.

L.M. WYANDOTTE

love is the best enemy.

i would have more enthusiasm in my companions, but their excuses silent secrets.

L.M. WYANDOTTE

the beauty of this woman is mysterious.
my eyes are locked on her inconceivable
soul.

LOVE THROUGH THE DARKNESS

the inability to smile a little is because the language of happiness is buried deep down in a dark place. and i'm speechless.

L.M. WYANDOTTE

the alley to laughter is dark and disturbing.

her eyes are mysterious and wonderful.

L.M. WYANDOTTE

her heart is illuminating, not strange.

i demand your hands when you want words, because my touch speaks in a tone so serious and loving, that words don't do enough.

L.M. WYANDOTTE

because of music we quiver all the time.

frankly, the eternal messages of the songs

will always speak when we can't or don't

want to.

darkness. the single vaccine for an artist.

L.M. WYANDOTTE

positively seduced by a surprising, obscene, and
admirable silliness. she is always able to
provide cheer. no matter what. and for that.
i am forever grateful.

LOVE THROUGH THE DARKNESS

in the end it'll cause pain. or it'll cause happiness. if you never start, you'll never know.

L.M. WYANDOTTE

> my love is magic. it'll make you think.
> it'll make you smile. but, most importantly,
> it'll keep you interested.

LOVE THROUGH THE DARKNESS

her and i came together like whiskey and ice.
she melted into me. and we became one.

L.M. WYANDOTTE

when i feel half-empty, i fill the glass
to the top.

how many times are you gonna believe his bullshit? that's how many more times you can expect to get let down and cry.

no man is worth the rest of your life if you're unhappy. even if you have a beautiful smile.

LOVE THROUGH THE DARKNESS

learn from the process. and the result.
bottle to body. hand to hand. cigarette
to lungs. heart to heart. all have pros
and cons. so does love. but, not when you
love the right one.

L.M. WYANDOTTE

if i defeated all my demons, who would

i drink with?

i will never forget her. her name is
branded into my heart because it belongs
to her.

and just like that. we were over before

we started.

LOVE THROUGH THE DARKNESS

watching you stay with him, is like you
asking for a cinder block as you tread
water.

L.M. WYANDOTTE

i'd starve so she could eat.
i'd be sober so she could drink.
her happiness is all i need.
to make my life complete.

LOVE THROUGH THE DARKNESS

my love is a gift and a curse.
if you have it, it's all yours.
when you fuck it up, you'll remind
yourself every day you'll never
experience another like it.

L.M. WYANDOTTE

heartbreak is the closest
to dying while still breathing.

sometimes i pour a drink. then i take
a sip each time i think of a great
memory of you. i go through a bottle
so quick.

L.M. WYANDOTTE

best and worst thing you can do
is think "what if?".

our rome wasn't built in a day.
but, it took you less than an
hour to destroy it.

L.M. WYANDOTTE

take another drag as the letters
appear on the paper. exhale. flick
away the ash and finish the drink.
another great day of typing sad
poems. just living the dream.

she wore winter so well. the coldness vanished when she smiled. it brought sunshine. even at night.

L.M. WYANDOTTE

to know love as i have, is to stand outside the lottery office that has locked doors waiting for it to open, holding a winning ticket.

her pearls moved as fast as
her breaths.

the shadows of the vibrations around
us murmured slowly. it must be impossible
when you're in a hurry to be subtle with
a kiss. these experiences give her lips
irresponsible fun.

the smile on the outside is the mask

for screaming on the inside.

i've seen the end of my world several times. then i wake up the next morning, take a breath and realize "it's not over yet".

LOVE THROUGH THE DARKNESS

if it ain't broke, leave it the fuck alone.

easiest way to torture a poet:
tell them you're interested in them.
because they'll wonder "why?".

when i'm lost, i open a bottle and
ask for directions.

L.M. WYANDOTTE

you got one shot at my love.
think when you reach the fork.

when she pours her heart out,
all i ask for is a refill.

L.M. WYANDOTTE

i want to hold her and stop time.
so i could decide for it to be
an actual forever hug.

LOVE THROUGH THE DARKNESS

she let go of me. so i never let go of

the drink.

sometimes i dip my toe into the deep end. but, haven't gone off it yet.

drunks have the best advice because
they don't have the best life.

L.M. WYANDOTTE

no one deserves pain and suffering.
but, you gotta go through some pain
and suffering to find out
what you deserve.

only sad clowns and statues don't have

to fake it.

L.M. WYANDOTTE

unless you're bringing great vibes
and whiskey, stay the fuck away.

LOVE THROUGH THE DARKNESS

if you felt my love. i mean my love,
not just me. know you made a short list.

L.M. WYANDOTTE

she's my cheese in the maze of life.

i may run out of time.
my love will never run out
for those who have felt it.

L.M. WYANDOTTE

in every bar are the smartest and
dumbest people. some are the same.

is it strange to love someone that is

now a stranger?

L.M. WYANDOTTE

i only feel the weight on my shoulders

on the dark days.

she is a rainstorm of love. and i'm
gonna soak up every drop.

L.M. WYANDOTTE

my love that burns for her outshines

the sun.

hearing someone's last breath will
change you forever.

L.M. WYANDOTTE

when it's raining, i either want
whiskey and wild sex or coffee
and cuddling. probably one and
then the other.

LOVE THROUGH THE DARKNESS

i spend more time thinking about her

than time allows.

i have moments when i don't think
there's anything that can pull me
back up. but. there she is.

i look forward to each day because
of her. even if i don't get to
see her.

she's the woman i fall to my knees for.
she's the woman i stand up for.
she's the woman i lose sleep for.
she's the woman that makes my time worthwhile.
she's the woman this smile is for.
she's the woman i will always give for.
she's the woman that in no way makes me feel poor.
she's the woman i will forever adore.
she will know these things from my words and more.

if my demons come out, it's to have a drink.

L.M. WYANDOTTE

false love is a non-alcoholic beer.

her smile was smoke. her words were mirrors.

L.M. WYANDOTTE

same as a breeze passes, so do thoughts
of getting back with an ex.

love is a shadow. of a past or current one.

L.M. WYANDOTTE

i quit saying i love you because i fixed

a broken record.

i caught her red-handed with the heart
of another man. but, i gave her the knife.

i don't need eyes to see her. she doesn't
need to be near to feel my love.

sometimes i drink to numb the pain of where

my heart once was.

L.M. WYANDOTTE

sometimes life is shit. just smile and
put a cherry on top.

i want to be comfortably numb in love.

humpty dumpty ain't shit compared to my heart.

if you look into my eyes,

those lips are mine.

L.M. WYANDOTTE

many nights i've drank brown and bled black. occasionally, my lips will be red.

i have secrets. most don't know them. if the people that knew me knew the secrets, they'd prolly wonder where the hell the smile on my face comes from.

L.M. WYANDOTTE

my feelings don't mean anything if she

is unhappy.

everyday with her is a great day. no matter what happens. because the day was spent with her.

in my dark moments. in my dark days. she
is my light. every. single. time.

LOVE THROUGH THE DARKNESS

i will endure any amount of pain so not a
single tear falls down her face.

L.M. WYANDOTTE

if you're gonna come into my darkness be prepared. hope you don't scare easy.

each day is spent as a HAPPYFACE SADFACE clown.

L.M. WYANDOTTE

if i can't have her, i may as well have nothing at all.

each day is the best and worst day of my life.

L.M. WYANDOTTE

one look in her brown eyes and all my

pain is gone.

i will never be able to tell someone i love you. i will never be able to say iloveyou enough to her.

L.M. WYANDOTTE

i can't love her enough. by my standard.

LOVE THROUGH THE DARKNESS

i'm living my life. i'm missing the life
i could be living with her.

a kiss on her neck. the smell of her hair.
i'm not sure who is more turned on.
me or her.

she is the reason my day begins.
she is also the reason i don't want
the day to end.

L.M. WYANDOTTE

try a little tenderness. and whiskey too.

my heart is locked up. only she has the key.

L.M. WYANDOTTE

watching my life from beginning to end
will be like the best mystery science
theater 3000 episode ever, if i get to commentate.

LOVE THROUGH THE DARKNESS

i kneel before her. blindfolded with my heart in hand. i say to her "do with it what you wish." you ever loved someone that much?

L.M. WYANDOTTE

the heart strings she tugs on are

lubricated with whiskey.

if i speak in her ear low and slow, that's
how her clothes will move.

L.M. WYANDOTTE

i am committed to her. my money. my love. my time. my effort. my breath. my blood. my organs. my everything. that's what she is to me. so, that's why all mine is hers.

she is a beautiful bottle of whiskey.
amazing curves. dark everything.
skin. hair. eyes. i want to take the
top of her off. drink all she has to
give. become intoxicated by her from
head to toe.

L.M. WYANDOTTE

the only thing better than a glass of

whiskey is the next one.

love is currently the only word i can use to singularly represent all of my positive thoughts and feelings regarding her. however, the word love doesn't do those thoughts and feelings justice. on a scale of 1 to 10, the word love is a 1. she deserves a 10. every. single. day. that's why i will forever be in debt to her. each day i work to be a better me. for her.

sadness doesn't look good on her. which
is why i won't ever help apply it.

i miss her. the her she keeps hidden from everyone else. the version of herself i fell in love with. the one that keeps me smiling on days of darkness. i wonder if she misses her too.

i imagine hell to be like society, except
only filled with unhappy people that
only see the bad in everything.

LOVE THROUGH THE DARKNESS

you're never alone. you always have
yourself. if that's not enough to
get started, then you're too dependent
on someone or something.

don't waste too much time thinking

about how much time you have.

when she is within sight, my eyes
don't wander. unless they're up
and down at her.

L.M. WYANDOTTE

the love i have for her is overpowering. at times it cripples me because of the weight on my shoulders and the pressure on my chest. but, she tells me "i feel the same" at that point we both knew we were always gonna be 50/50.

LOVE THROUGH THE DARKNESS

i don't want her to be anyone other than who she is. i didn't fall in love with her because i want her to be someone else.

your actions were a hurricane.

no budget could fit the repair bill.

my heart only beats for her.

L.M. WYANDOTTE

i tasted a love that is indescribable. a love that i now thirst for each day. and if i die of dehydration because of waiting, then so be it. there is no substitute for this love.

there is an immediate brick wall in front of me. i'm left with just enough air in my lungs to live. these things happen. every time i see her.

L.M. WYANDOTTE

just as a mountain can stare at the sun and moon, i could look at her forever. and always be smiling.

i forget what day it is. the time. the month.
for the moment i see her. time doesn't stand
still and neither does my heart.

L.M. WYANDOTTE

this left hand is still waiting for your right hand. so we can have our first dance. if time comes and i'm on my deathbed, my hand will still be out. waiting for yours.

LOVE THROUGH THE DARKNESS

science could erase her memory from my
brain. but, never from my soul.

L.M. WYANDOTTE

just the thought of her warms my heart

and soul on the coldest days.

there was a time my heart was turned to
stone. it's still stone, she just made
it warm.

L.M. WYANDOTTE

i get paid to work. nobody pays me to care.
that's my only job i can't be fired from.
because i can't collect unemployment.

death doesn't scare me. not that i welcome it. the death of others before me is what scares me most. when my time comes, i only want laughs around me. no tears. too many tears have been shed in my life. i don't want any shed for me because i passed. i want laughs because of the times people had with me.

don't handcuff a woman to bring her down.
you're not going to make your life better
by making hers worse. both will be made
worse. it's a lose-lose.

LOVE THROUGH THE DARKNESS

the only time you really organize your
life is when you write your will.

L.M. WYANDOTTE

each day is the best day and the worst day of my life. best because i'm alive. worst because i am alive and she is not.

LOVE THROUGH THE DARKNESS

my smile is mostly for show. an impression of how i want you to think my life is going. also, sometimes so you'll leave me the fuck alone.

L.M. WYANDOTTE

don't take life too seriously. i mean wear
your seatbelt. look both ways before you
cross the street. but, don't overthink your
day to the point you didn't really do anything.
call that guy/girl. take the shot. apply for
a job. tell the truth. love with all your heart
with whomever YOU want to be with. be happy.
if you're not, then find out why and fix it.
one life. make yours count for you first
then others.

air, food, water, and her. if i don't have the last, then the first three are useless.

love a woman for her intelligence, personality, sense of humor etc. and she will never be unattractive.

LOVE THROUGH THE DARKNESS

to hold her would be holding my why.
why i get out of bed.
why i keep moving forward.
why i keep bettering myself.
why i keep breathing.
because without her, why do anything?

L.M. WYANDOTTE

you can buy her diamonds.
you can buy her a house.
you can buy her a car.
you can buy her clothes.
however, the heart, soul, and love
aren't for sale. quit trying to bid
on them. it's just pissing her off.

best and worst way to address a situation: think.

L.M. WYANDOTTE

not too long after i pour a drink,
i pour out part of my soul on paper.

LOVE THROUGH THE DARKNESS

not sure she will ever know how much
i love her and how many times she
saved me without knowing.

L.M. WYANDOTTE

she went too soon. i'll never know why. even if someone told me, i wouldn't believe them. i would only believe her. but. she can't tell me. maybe one day.

i don't need someone to hold my hand.
but if i do, i want her to be the one.
because she is the one.

L.M. WYANDOTTE

there was an explosion. planets, galaxies, and stars formed. the next time an event like that occurred was when her lips met mine.

she sits playing with her hair, because she's
nervous. she sits thinking beautiful thoughts
from a mind filled with overthinking. she
smiles. she blinks long lashes with
pretty eyes in between. all the while,
not knowing i have been admiring her since
that first time these eyes saw her.

L.M. WYANDOTTE

my time. my effort. my love. my loyalty. my trust. my support. my money. all hers. her heart is filled with me. more than a fair trade.

took me a long time to find her.
which explains why waiting for her
doesn't require thought.

L.M. WYANDOTTE

the clock ticks unless she is near.

LOVE THROUGH THE DARKNESS

if the story ends and her and i
aren't together, then fuck the author.

L.M. WYANDOTTE

i'm never going to tell you that i love you more or better than someone before me. but, my love will be different. and for that reason, it'll be unlike those before me. i'm not competing with someone else, just myself from the day before. that's the person i want to love you more and better than.

when she walks into the room, sometimes
i kneel at her feet. she needs to be
reminded she is a goddess. and has power
over me like no other.

L.M. WYANDOTTE

love isn't being a punching bag.

i wanted to be your breath of fresh air,
but you wouldn't walk away from the smoke.

L.M. WYANDOTTE

too many people forget, life is a game. some have cheat codes, some run out of quarters.

i'd rather be alone if i can't be with her. nobody went to california for silver.

L.M. WYANDOTTE

flowers grow in the valley of darkness too.

some people are trees of positivity.

some people are assholes with chainsaws.

L.M. WYANDOTTE

if you love a woman, it better be with everything you have. everything. if not, then leave her the fuck alone.

if you love her halfway, expect half of
her heart. if that.

there is a reflection when i look in her
eyes. it is as if i can see myself as she
does. i'm not sure if it's because of the
smile on her face, her relaxed body, or the
ease at which her hands come to me. whatever
this is. i love it.

if you can't be man enough to surrender
to her, why the hell would she surrender
to you?

she and i may not get to talk. she and i may not get to touch. but, i know she keeps her love for me hidden and protected. nothing can destroy that love. not words or actions from others, because they don't know its strength. not even time can put out the flame. it burns for eternity. from this life into the next.

LOVE THROUGH THE DARKNESS

i am hypnotized by THOSE pretty eyes. the trance intensifies as i attempt to take in the rest of her beauty. a rapid pounding builds in my chest as my heart attempts to explode from producing too much love. then she speaks and all i can say is...iloveyou.

L.M. WYANDOTTE

record slowly playing al green. your hand in mine. your head on my chest. our feet shuffling to our own rhythm. so close our hearts share the same beat. the red wine and your red lips have me intoxicated. don't pull away. let me pretend i'll have you forever.

i'd rather live with failed attempts than successful regrets.

L.M. WYANDOTTE

so many parties of one on the waitlist in the restaurant of love. sadly, some are in a relationship.

i wonder if she thinks of me. if she imagines our life together. imagines the love i'd give. i imagine she isn't given permission to have an imagination. imagine that.

L.M. WYANDOTTE

when she walks out the door, the glass
is always half full. after i find the
ring left on the floor, the glass is always
half full.

LOVE THROUGH THE DARKNESS

life is a constant struggle.
struggle for knowledge.
struggle for love.
struggle for acceptance.
too often, people think they're
struggling alone.

L.M. WYANDOTTE

her eyes could start or stop a war.
imagine what her words could do.

LOVE THROUGH THE DARKNESS

those bad times you experienced in the past should make you not want to repeat them. so, don't make them happen for others. especially those that want the best for you. and you'll be able to figure out who those people are. their heart and soul may be guarded like yours. but, eventually the walls come down. and when they do, be ready to exchange hearts.

L.M. WYANDOTTE

death causes life's clock to stop ticking.

a person's life can only live on once

it's stopped.

L.M. WYANDOTTE

i live with death every day.

LOVE THROUGH THE DARKNESS

when the sand runs out of my hourglass,
i want to feel her lips as the last grain
drops. for whatever comes after, will start
with love and her.

L.M. WYANDOTTE

don't think it's just your looks that turn me on. the way you dress. the different ways you wear your hair. the way you sing your favorite songs. the way you smile when something makes you happy. simply, the way you're you. that's why i love you.

now or in 10 years, these arms will be
open and ready to hold you again.

L.M. WYANDOTTE

i don't drink to escape reality.
i escape reality to drink.

life without love is not life.

L.M. WYANDOTTE

her love is my life support.

some of the best and worst time spent is

in your head.

L.M. WYANDOTTE

once i get to your soul, i'll be with you

for the rest of your lives.

LOVE THROUGH THE DARKNESS

there's a lot i can do with these hands.
i can build, write, mix, grab, hold,
carry, play, work, and the list goes on.
but without her, they're just a pair of
empty hands.

my last breath will be used to tell her

"i love you." *fade to black*

don't do that. don't hurt yourself for someone that wouldn't do the same for you. that's not sacrifice or compromise. that's suicide of the soul.

L.M. WYANDOTTE

love is wanting someone to
see/feel/understand/know/hear
you as you wish you could.

LOVE THROUGH THE DARKNESS

don't do it for money. if that's the only
reason, you'll regret it later. you may
not think so now, or before you do it, but
will at some point when you realize what was
the trade. and then you realize it was a raw
deal, one you were on the wrong end of.
but, then you get better at making deals, or
at minimum being an intermediary of good ones.

L.M. WYANDOTTE

just as i breathe, loving her is natural.

LOVE THROUGH THE DARKNESS

a blind person can see clearer than a
person with 20/20 vision.

L.M. WYANDOTTE

my hands have both held life as it came into the world. and. as it left. in that window of time, my life also began and ended.

the love i give her is an extension of my soul.

there's always a reason. look for the light. somewhere. in someone, something, if not yourself. don't give up. ever.

LOVE THROUGH THE DARKNESS

i don't need time on my side because
i have faith i will be with her.
if not in this life, then the next
one. and when we're together the
impact will be like a soul connection
version of the big bang.

L.M. WYANDOTTE

love without judgment. or don't
love at all. because once you
start judging it gets in the way
of love.

when i'm done with life, i'll let
death know. not the other way around

L.M. WYANDOTTE

i don't want bad thoughts. awful thoughts. thoughts on events i can't experience. thoughts about people i can't be with. even the happiest thoughts i have can't keep the bad thoughts away. they are just kept at bay. just gotta take the good with the bad. and that's life in one sentence.

act tough. but when the sun sets, there's no food, no cigarettes, no drinks. that's when the loneliness will sink in. all the way to your bones. that is when you will miss him/her. that is when that one, your one will be the only thing on your mind. because nothing else will fill that void.

L.M. WYANDOTTE

my love/appreciation/care/respect/admiration
for her every day makes valentine's day seem
like another day on the calendar.

lit candles, warm blankets, rain on the
roof, and the sound of her voice. all combined
to make an amazing time.

L.M. WYANDOTTE

the energy in the connection between her and i is something unknown to science. physical, mental, and emotional energy even without touch or sometimes sight. it's similar to love, but not the same thing.

LOVE THROUGH THE DARKNESS

her love is the rain and shine i need. to grow. as a human. and as a man. without her love i am malnourished.

L.M. WYANDOTTE

the sun rises in morning and sets in the evening. but, my love for her never goes away.

each and every day, i breathe for her.

L.M. WYANDOTTE

i can't do what she does.

even magicians are confused.

LOVE THROUGH THE DARKNESS

each time i see the sunshine i am happy.
because i get another day to spend loving
her.

L.M. WYANDOTTE

tears in her eyes are daggers in my heart.

heels and pearls. one of my favorite outfits of hers.

L.M. WYANDOTTE

each day i learn another reason why i love her.

LOVE THROUGH THE DARKNESS

time moves on, but, my love for her won't.

L.M. WYANDOTTE

staying in your comfort zone is for hamsters.

if you don't love her, i mean really love
her with your heart, soul, and breath then
fuck off and don't waste anymore of her time.
because she can't get back what's been spent on you.

L.M. WYANDOTTE

her love is my breath and blood.

i don't want to be a better man for me.
i want to be a better man for her.

L.M. WYANDOTTE

bottles will empty.
tears will dry.
my soul will never
forget her and her love.

tell me what you love
about me. when you ask me the
same about you, i will say
"everything you are. what i
can see and what i can't."

L.M. WYANDOTTE

love is obese.

LOVE THROUGH THE DARKNESS

the moment when you wake up and realize
you get another day to live. your eyes
open and you realize you're still breathing.
the feeling you have when you realize those
moments, is what i feel each second loving her.

L.M. WYANDOTTE

love without her is
life without breathing.

LOVE THROUGH THE DARKNESS

she is the center of my universe. which is why i can't live without my heart and soul. because she makes it continue.

L.M. WYANDOTTE

is her love worth your life?
if you hesitated, then you're
not all in. be all in or not at all.

i want to make love to her. physically, verbally, mentally, and emotionally. even when she isn't in front of me.

days spent waiting. waiting for everything. love. death. money. time. holidays. births. happiness. sadness. the worst part is the waiting makes the present irrelevant.

L.M. Wyandotte is a prolific poet who writes on the theme of love and loss. He has been writing for many years, and considers his life as still being written.

LOVE THROUGH THE DARKNESS is his fourth book.

See more of L.M. Wyandotte's work at:

instagram: @l.m.wyandotte
twitter: @lmwyandotte
TikTok: @l.m.wyandotte
Facebook: L.M. Wyandotte

www.ingramcontent.com/pod-product-compliance
Lightning Source LLC
Chambersburg PA
CBHW070848050426
42453CB00012B/2088